Photo of hurricane
Danny 1984

Chapter 1

Hurricane David

August 3-4

Had winds of 95 mph

Winds gust of 100 mph

I was just 3 years old when hurricane I just remembered we went to our cousin house . it was windy .

Chapter 2

Hurricane Dennis

August 16-19 1981

Winds of 40 mph

Orlando Florida

Winds sw at 20 MPH

Gust at 32 MPH

I don't really remember any thing much with storm

Chapter 3

Hurricane Barry

August 24-25 1983

Winds of 45 mph

It was a tropical storm when hit palm bay to Tampa bay

I had to stay inside

I remember I was wftv weather reports

It windy and rainy

Chapter 4

Major hurricane Diane

September 8-10 1984

Winds 45 MPH

Was near 65 miles from cape Canaveral

3.2 feet waves

Some rain and wind.

Chapter 5

Tropical storm Isidore

July 22-24

40 MPH winds

West Melbourne to Daytona Beach

6.5 inches of rain

This storm I don't remember much it rain alot

Chapter 6

Hurricane Bob

July 22-24 1985

50 MPH wind gusts 65 MPH

It was tropical storm when it hit Florida

It wasn't that bad some wind and rain

I had stay inside and play inside

Chapter 7

Hurricane Danny

August 15 1985

Louisiana / Mississippi

We went to Texas to visit my grandma

I remember somebody told us we might to leave early

To miss the storm .

But when we got a hotel in Louisiana and turned the TV

We found out it was heading our way . I think we leave early .

I always called this hurricane the storm that chased us.

Chapter 8

Hurricane Elena

August 31- September 1 1985

125 MPH 953 mlb cat.3

It did double loop in the gulf of Mexico

It was long couple of days for Florida

I remember my parents was ready to leave the trailer .

We didn't have to.

Chapter 9

Hurricane Floyd

October 12 1987

Melbourne Florida

Winds 22 MPH gust 32 mph

This Storm was very wet storm some winds not bad.

Chapter 10

Tropical storm Chris

August 27-28 1988

Winds 40 MPH

Melbourne winds 25 MPH gust 44 MPH

Chapter 11

Tropical storm keith

October 10-11

25mph in Melbourne

40 MPH

It was windy most of the day

It's was windy fall day cloudy cool

Those days was fun for us.

Chapter 12

Tropical storm anna

July 30- august 2 1990

Hit as a depression when hit fla

Chapter 13

Tropical storm Marco

October 10-11 1990

1003.2 mb

Chapter 14

Tropical storm Anna

July 30- August 2 1991

Chapter 15

Major hurricane Andrew

August 24 1992

Cat.5 hit Florida

That storm most scary storm I went through

I remember sitting out side listening to the radio for hurricane

reports

Every time they said a report it got worse.

I can tell u we had at least tropical storm winds in Melbourne

fla.

Watching the out bands of hurricane Andrew was interested.

We had friends moved from Dade and Miami they went through the

whole hurricane winds the was scared to death.

Chapter 16

Hurricane Gordon

November 16-20 1994

29 MPH winds gust 36 MPH in palm bay fla.

6.60 inches rain

   I remember a thunderstorm part of hurricane Gordon

Made our trailer shook very hard. it scared me very bad.

I always thought there was tornado went close to us.

Chapter 17

Hurricane Erin

August 1-2 1995

75 mph

985 mlb in Melbourne Fla

Wind 75 MPH

Gust in Melbourne Florida 66 MPH

Hurricane Erin we wasn't expecting her to hit us .she a slow
mover. Put when she hit very heavy rain and winds the most part
of the storm rain was the out bands of the storm. Never seen a
storm back part was worse the front part of a storm.

Chapter 18

Tropical storm Jerry

August 23-25 1995

Very rainy all day winds wasn't that bad.

Chapter 19

Tropical storm Josephine

October 7 1996

Chapter 20

Major hurricane Mitch

October 5 1998

Was a tropical storm when hit Fla

Melbourne Florida 998.3 25mph

Wind gusts 30 MPH 1.54 inches of rain

Chapter 21

Hurricane Floyd

September 14-15 1999

Went pass Florida

About 95 m from cape Canaveral Fla

Melbourne fla winds 40 MPH gust 59 MPH

This storm didn't turn til the last minute. i remember putting up
wood on the house and shutters on one my friends the trailer. I
remember watching the leading edge of the the hurricane started
to turn north.

We had to convince my friend father to get out of the trailer it
took for hours to do that. But we was glad it flood the trailer
park.

There was a lot of wind and rain that night.

Chapter 22

Hurricane Gabrielle

September 14-15 2001

25 MPH gust at 35 MPH

4.18 inches

The storm Hit couple days after 9/11

Some wind and rain

Chapter 23

Tropical storm Edouard

September 5 2002

Weak tropical storm.

Not much big happen

Chapter 24

2003 tropical storm Henri

Some rain and wind.

Chapter 25

2004 tropical storm Bonnie

August 12 2004

Hit Florida day before Charley hit

Chapter 26

Major hurricane Charley

August 13 2004

Cat.4 145 MPH

Melbourne Florida 1010.5 mlb

Winds 29 MPH

Gust 39 MPH

1.44 inches of rain

Orlando Florida 984.2

Winds 57 mph

Gust 71 MPH

2.37 inches of rain

I was watching my niece and nephew and watching the weather

reports and 1pm wftv told us it was turning toward Orlando area

and it got much stronger than it was couple hours .it was getting

stronger too. I had to call my mom to ask what we was going to do

we decided

To to closed the antique store early and the kids the moms house

Get ready . it was just like three hours get ready . we had 9

people at parents house

I remember one gust came through the back yard and all the trees bend over and I can see the houses behind our house. A lot of wind. Some rain.

Hurricane Frances

September 4-6 2004

Melbourne fla

995.9 mlb

Winds 65 MPH

7.95 inches of rain

Vero beach

Winds 49 mph

Gust of 71 MPH

8.11 inches of rain in Melbourne fla wfo

Palm bay fla 7.27 inches of rain

This storm was so slow to move when hit Florida

The power went out the couple hours.

We had 13 people in my parents house.

The wind was strong most of the first day and half

It took at least three days the rain to quite.

And took 8 days get power to turn on

we had the chance to go out side .

We cooked on the grill

That was a very long hurricane

Chapter 28

Major hurricane Jeanne

September 25 -26 2004

Melbourne fla

Winds 52 MPH gust of 68 MPH

This storm did a loop then came back hit the same spot Frances

hit two weeks latter the was stronger palm bay had to have winds

over

110 MPH winds because I remember the house walls start to shack

alot

I never felt the house shack any other hurricane.

We had power longer then Frances but around 2am it went off

It was another 8 days with electronic .

The government did a good job too help all the people in Florida.

We did stay a few nights at the antique shop .

Chapter 29

Hurricane Ophelia

September 6-7 2005

Patrick air force Base

Winds 26 MPH gust 34 MPH

2.03 inches of rain

Melbourne Fla

1.96 inches of rain

Was of the east coast

Just a rainy storm

Chapter 30

Tropical storm Tammy

October 5 2005

Chapter 31

Major hurricane Wilma

October 25 2005

Melbourne fla

Gust 67 MPH 4.25 inches of rain

Palm bay 5.47 inches of rain

Melbourne beach fla 5.14 inches

Palm bay fla coop

Gust 65 MPH

This storm was one storm I never thought I would be in

The winds was so Strong it hit south Florida but the whole

State got this storm .

There was tornadoes in downtown Melbourne fla

I went there to check on the antique store the u seen

Blowing rain .u couldn't see the streets or the stores in front .

And wouldn't try to open the doors again in that kinda storm.

It will ripe the from u hands

The awesome thing I seen it was after the storm went past it

clear and cold .

U can the clouds clear it was beautiful.

Chapter 32

Tropical storm Albert

June 13 2006

Melbourne fla 2010.5 mlb

31 MPH gust of 49 MPH

2.32 inches of rain

Chapter 33

Hurricane Ernesto

August 30-31 2006

Winds 25 gust 33mph

3.06 inches of rain

Chapter 34

Tropical storm Barry

June 2 2007

Melbourne Florida

6.03 inches or rain

Tropical storm fay

August 18-22 2009

Flooding in palm bay and Melbourne fla

Melbourne 6 nw 21.88 inches of rain

Melbourne 7nw 20.50 inches of rain

Melbourne windover farms 27.65 of rain

Palm bay 21.00 inches of rain

Fay was the longest and wet storm I ever went it seemed it a week

to get rid of her

It wasn't the wind that was the problem

It was the the rain it keep going for days.

We had power all the time

Put it was boring staying it side for days

We went to the antique store

On the trip there

We seen cars stuck in ditches

The Rhodes park lake was flooding over the road .

Minton road was so Florida .

Chapter 36

Tropical storm Debby

June 25-27 2012

Winds 25 MPH

Gust was 33mph

Chapter 37

Tropical storm Andrea

Melbourne Florida

1005.8

Gust 34 MPH